I0817564

MODERN STARS

TOM HOLLAND

by Carla Mooney

An Imprint of Abdo Publishing
abdobooks.com

ABDOBOOKS.COM

Published by Abdo Publishing, a division of ABDO, PO Box 398166, Minneapolis, Minnesota 55439.

Printed in China.
102025
012026

Cover Photo: Christopher Polk/WWD/Getty Images
Interior Photos: Shutterstock Images, 5; Columbia Pictures/Entertainment Pictures/Alamy, 7; Todd Williamson/Getty Images for CinemaCon/Getty Images Entertainment/Getty Images, 8; David M. Benett/WireImage/Dave Benett Collection/Getty Images, 13, 40; Sampajano Anizza/Shutterstock Images, 15; Dave M. Benett/Dave Benett Collection/Getty Images, 19, 22; Moviestore Collection Ltd/Alamy, 25, 29, 36–37; Pictorial Press Ltd/Alamy, 26, 61; Ian West/PA Images/Getty Images, 31; Debby Wong/Shutterstock Images, 34; Plan B Entertainment/Album/Alamy, 43; Aidan Monaghan/Photo 12/Keep Your Head/Plan B Entertainment/Alamy, 44; Columbia Pictures/Marvel Entertainment/Album/Alamy, 47; Robert Nickelsberg/Getty Images News/Getty Images, 48; Marvel Studios/Columbia Pictures/Moviestore Collection Ltd/Alamy, 52; Chuck Zlotnick/Columbia Pictures/Marvel Studios/Photo 12/Alamy, 55; Juan Naharro Gimenez/WireImage/Getty Images, 57; Mike Marsland/WireImage/Getty Images, 58; BFA/Walt Disney Studios/Alamy, 63; RW/MediaPunch/IPX/AP Images, 66; Angela Weiss/AFP/Getty Images, 70; Bronx Moving Co./Nine Stories Productions/Album/Alamy, 73; The Hideaway Entertainment/AGBO/Album/Alamy, 75; Columbia Pictures/Album/Alamy, 80; Marvel Entertainment/Moviestore Collection Ltd/Alamy, 82–83; Matt Kennedy/Photo 12/7e Art/Columbia Pictures/Marvel Studios/Alamy, 87; Araya Doheny/Getty Images Entertainment/Getty Images, 91; Apple TV+/Regency Enterprises/Album/Alamy, 94; Klára Šimonová/Getty Images Entertainment/Getty Images, 97; Euan Cherry/Getty Images for University of St Andrews/Getty Images Entertainment/Getty Images, 98

Editor: Laura Stickney
Series Designer: Karli Hughes

Library of Congress Control Number: 2025939785

PUBLISHER'S CATALOGING-IN-PUBLICATION DATA

Names: Mooney, Carla, author.
Title: Tom Holland / by Carla Mooney
Description: Minneapolis, Minnesota: Abdo Publishing, 2026 | Series: Modern stars | Includes online resources and index.
Identifiers: ISBN 9781098298135 (lib. bdg.) | ISBN 9798384931935 (ebook)
Subjects: LCSH: Holland, Tom, 1996- --Juvenile literature. | Actors--Great Britain--Biography--Juvenile literature. | Motion picture actors and actresses--Great Britain--Biography--Juvenile literature. | Superhero films--Juvenile literature. | Spiderman (Fictitious character)--Juvenile literature.
Classification: DDC 791.4302--dc23

CONTENTS

CHAPTER ONE

THE ROLE OF A LIFETIME

British actor Tom Holland grew up as a huge Spider-Man fan. As a child, he owned many Spider-Man costumes. He slept on Spider-Man bedsheets. He even dressed up as Spider-Man for parties. So when Marvel Studios announced in early 2015 that it was recasting the iconic superhero for a new film franchise, the young actor called his agents and begged them to get him an audition for the role.

Once he was given the green light to send in an audition tape, Holland filmed himself doing flips. The actor had trained in gymnastics as a child and wanted to show off his skills for Marvel. While introducing

Tom Holland did a total of eight auditions before landing the role of Peter Parker. During some of his auditions, he improvised flips and other acrobatic moves. >>

himself on camera, Holland did backflips, side flips, and front flips.

Holland was one of more than 1,500 teens who auditioned for the coveted role of Spider-Man, otherwise known as teenager Peter Parker. The audition process lasted more than five months. Holland did multiple auditions, including five audition tapes and several screen tests.[1] A screen test is a filmed audition that filmmakers use to decide whether a particular actor is right for a role.

Screen tests are usually done later in the audition process, when filmmakers have narrowed down the number of actors they are considering. During a screen test, an actor may be asked to say certain lines or express specific emotions. Sometimes multiple actors perform in a screen test so filmmakers can evaluate how well they work together.

THOR'S APPROVAL

When Holland was auditioning for the role of Spider-Man, he called another superhero for help. He had previously worked with Chris Hemsworth, who plays Thor in several Marvel Studios films, on a movie called *In the Heart of the Sea.* Holland asked Hemsworth to put in a good word for him with the Spider-Man producers. Hemsworth joked that he'd tell Marvel that Holland could never remember his lines. But when Hemsworth called Marvel, he gave a glowing recommendation of Holland and praised him as an extremely talented actor.

At one point, Holland flew to Atlanta, Georgia, for a screen test with Robert Downey Jr., who plays the role of Iron Man. "There was me and six other kids, and [Robert] Downey [Jr.] was there, so we all tested with Downey, which was crazy," Holland later said. "It's the best audition I've ever done, him and I were riffing off each other. My agents told me that Marvel likes you to learn the words exactly—you can't improvise. And then, on the first take, Downey just completely changed the scene."[2] Holland followed Downey's lead and improvised during the screen test.

Although Holland thought the screen test went well, he did not hear anything from Marvel right away. Finally, about six weeks later, Marvel invited the actor back to Atlanta for another screen test. This time, Holland performed a fight scene

In several Marvel Studios films, Robert Downey Jr.'s Iron Man acts as a mentor to Holland's Spider-Man. Since meeting in a 2015 audition, the two actors have developed a similar bond off-screen.

with Chris Evans, who plays Captain America. Holland told himself that even if he did not land the Spider-Man role, the experience of auditioning with stars such as Downey and Evans was worth it.

When Marvel's casting lead, Sarah Halley Finn, watched Holland's audition, she knew they had found the new Peter Parker. She told Marvel directors Joe Russo and Anthony Russo that they would love the young actor. Producers Kevin Feige and Amy Pascal were impressed with Holland's work in films such as *The Impossible*.

The Russos also thought that the young actor's gymnastics and dance skills could be beneficial for the role. Even Stan Lee, the cocreator of Spider-Man, gave his approval. He noted that Holland was the exact age

***From left to right*, director Jon Watts, Tom Holland, producer Amy Pascal, and Marvel Studios president Kevin Feige have collaborated on multiple films.**

and height that Lee had imagined when he first came up with Spider-Man.

STAN LEE

Stan Lee was an American comic book writer, editor, and publisher. While working at Marvel Comics, he cocreated beloved characters such as Spider-Man, Iron Man, Thor, and the Hulk. Lee's rich imagination and storytelling helped turn Marvel into a global powerhouse. Lee became a pop-culture legend, making cameo appearances in many Marvel films. Lee died in 2018.

SILENCE AND SURPRISE

Weeks passed, and Holland heard nothing about the role from anyone at Marvel Studios. He assumed the studio had chosen another actor. In June 2015, Holland was scrolling through Instagram on his phone. He noticed that Marvel had posted a cartoon image of Spider-Man on its account. The post instructed fans to visit the studio's website to discover who the next Spider-Man was.

Curious to see who had gotten the role, Holland opened his laptop while his dog sat next to him on his bed. He went to the Marvel website and began reading the studio's announcement. Stunned, he read, "We would like to introduce our new Spider-Man, Tom Holland."[3]

Holland was so surprised that he accidentally flipped his computer, and it fell off the bed and broke. He ran downstairs and shouted to his family that he had gotten the Spider-Man role. At first, Holland's brother suspected the news was a hoax. "My brother, Harry, who's quite tech-savvy, was like, 'No. There's no way that's real. They would have called you. They've been hacked,'" Holland said.[4]

Holland quickly called his agents. They had seen the same announcement on the internet but had not talked to anyone from Marvel either. Then the president of Marvel Studios called Holland to confirm what he had read online. Holland was going to be the next Spider-Man.

In a statement, Pascal discussed the decision to cast Holland. "Sony, Marvel, Kevin, and I all knew that for Peter Parker, we had to find a vibrant, talented young actor capable of embodying one of the most well-known characters in the world," she said. "With Tom, we've found the perfect actor to bring Spider-Man's story into the Marvel Cinematic Universe."[5]

THE ORIGINAL SPIDER-MEN

Actor Tobey Maguire first brought Spider-Man to the big screen in three movies: *Spider-Man* in 2002, *Spider-Man 2* in 2004, and *Spider-Man 3* in 2007. His portrayal of Peter Parker was noted for having an engaging blend of awkwardness and charm. Actor Andrew Garfield later took over the iconic role in another Spider-Man series. He starred as Peter Parker in two films, *The Amazing Spider-Man* in 2012 and *The Amazing Spider-Man 2* in 2014. In 2021, Maguire and Garfield made surprise appearances in *Spider-Man: No Way Home*, acting alongside Holland.

Nineteen-year-old Holland would be the third actor to portray the web-slinging superhero in a major live-action film, following Tobey Maguire and Andrew Garfield. Holland would also be the youngest actor to play Spider-Man. Maguire was 26 years old when he was cast in the role, and Garfield was 27. Holland's casting meant that for the first time, a real teenager would play the teenage Spider-Man.

A CAREER-DEFINING MOMENT

For Holland, Spider-Man was the role of a lifetime. His casting was a surprise for some. Holland was a British teen growing up in London, England, making his way through school and exploring his interest in acting. While he had some experience working on movies, most of his previous acting had been in stage productions, such as *Billy Elliot: The Musical*.

Nevertheless, the young actor had shown great promise in his early career. His youthful earnestness, charisma, and slight awkwardness were qualities that made him the perfect choice for Peter Parker. In Holland, the filmmakers saw a teen who had the same infectious enthusiasm as his character. The high-profile role would change the trajectory of Holland's career forever.

CHAPTER TWO

EARLY YEARS

Thomas Stanley Holland was born on June 1, 1996, in Kingston upon Thames. This town is located about 12 miles (19 km) southwest of central London in England.[1] The eldest of four boys, Tom grew up in an artistic household. His father, Dominic Holland, is a stand-up comedian and writer. His mother, Nicola "Nikki" Holland, is a photographer.

From an early age, Tom loved to dance. His father remembers him as a toddler dancing to the Janet Jackson song "Together Again." Every time the song played, Tom danced. Around age nine, Tom enrolled in a hip-hop dance class at the Nifty Feet Dance School in Wimbledon, a suburb of London.

The school's founder, Lynne Page, was a choreographer who had trained actor Jamie Bell for his leading role in the hit movie *Billy Elliot*. It tells the

***From left to right*, Sam, Harry, Tom, and Paddy Holland have maintained close relationships since childhood. The brothers frequently attend premieres and events together.** >>

Disney · PIXAR
MISSING BRIDGE
TRAINEE
PATH OF
PIXAR

story of a talented young boy from a coal-mining family who discovers a passion for dance and ballet. Page also trained dancers for the West End theater production of *Billy Elliot: The Musical*. The West End is a London district known for its theaters.

In 2006, Tom's hip-hop class performed at the Richmond Dance Festival. A representative from London's Royal Ballet School noticed the young dancer there. The talent scout attended events across the country, searching for young actors and dancers to play Billy Elliot in the London stage production. It needed a constant supply of child actors to take over the role as the current actors grew too old for the part. The talent scout persuaded Page to send Tom to audition for the musical at London's Victoria Palace Theatre.

BILLY ELLIOT MOVIE

The film *Billy Elliot*, which came out in 2000, is set in an English coal-mining town during the 1984–85 miners' strike. It tells the story of 11-year-old Billy, who stumbles upon a ballet class and discovers a hidden talent and passion for dance. Despite his father's initial disapproval, Billy secretly pursues ballet and auditions for the Royal Ballet School. *Billy Elliot* received widespread critical acclaim. Critics praised its storytelling, powerful performances, and emotional depth. The film earned multiple award nominations, including three Academy Award nominations and 13 British Academy of Film and Television Arts (BAFTA) nominations.[2] It won several awards, including the BAFTA for Best British Film.

***Billy Elliot: The Musical* first premiered at London's Victoria Palace Theatre in 2005. The hit show went on to win more than 80 theater awards, including ten Tony Awards.**

Before the audition, Tom's father took him to see the musical. Dominic Holland thought the idea of his son joining the production and even playing the lead role seemed unthinkable. "There was just no way. No chance. Ballet, tap, singing, acting; Tom had never done any of these things. He had never even been cast in any of his school plays," said Dominic.[3]

Just as his father predicted, Tom did not impress many of the talent evaluators at his *Billy Elliot* audition.

However, Tom caught the eye of Stephen Daldry, who had directed both the movie and the musical. Daldry liked Tom's presence onstage, his natural acting talent, and his ability to take direction. When the musical's choreographer pointed out that Tom had little dance experience, Daldry told the choreographer to teach him.

For the next two years, Tom trained in ballet, tap dance, and acrobatics. At the time, the ten-year-old was attending the Donhead Preparatory School in Wimbledon. He practiced during his lunch hours at school and in his garage at home. Like many boys his age, Tom enjoyed playing rugby. But he had to give up the sport to focus on his dance lessons. The reaction from some of Tom's peers was not always positive. The young dancer was often bullied.

DYSLEXIA

When Tom was seven years old, doctors diagnosed him with dyslexia. This learning disability affects how the brain processes language and can cause difficulty with reading. Tom's parents enrolled him in a private school that would be able to give him the attention he needed to overcome the condition. Tom had trouble reading and writing as a kid. As an adult, the actor still makes spelling mistakes on social media. But he says that patience and preparation have helped him manage his dyslexia.

LONDON STAGE DEBUT

In June 2008, Tom debuted in the West End production of *Billy Elliot: The Musical*. At first, Tom played the role of Billy's best friend, Michael. The role eased Tom into the bright lights of the West End theater, laying the foundation for his stage career.

Actor Craig Gallivan, who played the role of Billy's older brother, Tony, in the musical, immediately noticed that Tom was special. "The children I was lucky enough to work with on *Billy Elliot* were all exceptional talents so it was something of an impossibility to stand out from that, but Tom did," he said. "For me, it was his connection to the dialogue. He had access to an emotional sensitivity that was way beyond his years."[4]

Within months, Tom landed the lead role of Billy Elliot. He was one of several young actors who rotated in the role. The United Kingdom has strict laws about how often children can work, so each Billy actor was limited to two or three shows a week.[5] Tom moved in to the Billy Elliot House in Ealing, London, with other kids in the show. Cast members lived in this house while rehearsals and performances were going on.

The child actors had school lessons in the morning, ate lunch, and went to stage rehearsals in the afternoons.

Training for the show was a lot of work. But for Tom, all the rehearsals, late nights, and early mornings were worth it.

On September 8, 2008, Tom made his debut as Billy Elliot onstage. His parents admitted they were nervous about their son taking on the production's lead role. "There are only fifteen minutes in the two-and-a-half-hour show when Billy is offstage. When Tom first played Billy, Nikki and I just couldn't watch," said Dominic.[6]

On the day of his debut, Tom developed tonsillitis. This condition causes a person's tonsils to become swollen. Determined not to let anyone down, Tom did not tell anyone he was sick.

He didn't want to miss the performance because he knew so many people were coming to see it. Tom was fantastic onstage that night, and no one noticed he was sick until the next day. He saw a doctor and was told to take the rest of the week off.

The experience left Tom with a nickname he did not like. "I got the nickname Sick Note, which frustrates me to my core, even today," Tom said in 2021. "I was too young to do that show. I was incredibly underdeveloped as a kid, and I would get sick, or I would be tired, or I would get injured, and I'd need to take a break because you're doing three shows a week, rehearsing every single day. Now as

As Billy Elliot, Tom became known for his stage presence, agility, and impressive dance skills. In 2010, the young actor told a reporter that the role helped him gain more confidence.

an actor I push through everything, because I'm not going to be Sick Note."[7]

A TWO-YEAR RUN

Tom's choreography in the show highlighted his skills in street-style dance and acrobatics. He dazzled audiences with his flips, including a no-hands forward flip. In the musical's signature dance number, "Electricity," Tom performed a backward flip while walking up a wall. The acrobatic move thrilled audiences at each show.

The musical ran for about two hours and 40 minutes each night, including a 15-minute intermission.[8] As Billy, Tom's longest offstage break was only seven minutes long.[9] The young actor admitted he usually spent that time practicing the words to the "Electricity" number so he would not forget them.

Tom spent nearly two years onstage as Billy Elliot. During that time, he did many interviews and television appearances. He quickly became known in the media for his sense of humor and friendly personality. When one newspaper reporter asked the young actor where he got his talent, Tom had a quick response ready. "My mum and dad joke about who I take after," he said. "I've seen them both dance and I have to say, there must have been a mix-up at the hospital."[10]

Despite his success onstage, Tom remained dedicated to his family and life at home. In the show's playbill, he dedicated his performance to his three younger brothers, Paddy and twins Sam and Harry. Tom's father spoke about how proud he was of his eldest son. "We are all so proud of Tom—nobody can take this away from him," he said. "It's one of the very few child parts which has the name in the show's title. Whatever else, he will always have been Billy Elliot. And yes, I can watch him now, because I know he can do it."[11]

In 2010, *Billy Elliot: The Musical* celebrated its fifth anniversary on the London stage. In March 2010, Tom and the other child actors playing Billy were invited to meet British prime minister Gordon Brown at 10 Downing Street, London. This is the official residence and government office of the British prime minister.

Tom was also selected to play the role of Billy in a special fifth-anniversary performance of the show, which took place on March 31, 2010. Legendary musician Elton John, who composed the music of *Billy Elliot: The Musical*, was in the audience for the anniversary show. He was impressed by Tom's performance in the lead role and said that he was blown away by the young actor's talent.

FOLLOWING IN TOM'S FOOTSTEPS

Two of Tom's younger brothers have followed him into acting. Harry Holland has appeared in a few movies with Tom, including *Spider-Man: No Way Home*. He has also stepped behind the camera, directing a short film called *Roses for Lily* in 2020. Tom's youngest brother, Paddy, is also an actor. He has appeared in several small movie and television roles. Sam Holland works as a chef in London. He served as Tom's personal chef during the filming of *Spider-Man: Far from Home*.

During the fifth-anniversary performance of *Billy Elliot* in 2010, 19 past and present Billy actors appeared onstage for a special finale. The actors celebrated with Elton John, *center*.

AN ENDING AND A BEGINNING

As with all the child actors who played Billy, Tom's time in the lead role eventually came to an end as he grew older. His last performance in the show was on May 29, 2010. Returning to school after playing Billy was not as easy as he had expected.

"I was coming back a West End lead—I was going to be the coolest kid in school! But it wasn't the case," Tom said. "I'd matured so much in a professional environment that when I went back to school, I was shocked how much more mature I was than my peers. I didn't really fit in."[12]

After two years on the stage, Tom was ready to slide back into life as a young teen at home. But soon, a phone call changed everything. A casting director wanted Tom to audition for a role in a Hollywood movie.

CHAPTER THREE

HOLLYWOOD'S CALLING

In 2010, Spanish film director J. A. Bayona was preparing for his next project, *The Impossible*. The movie is about a family who survives the 2004 Indian Ocean tsunami in Thailand. It is based on the real-life Álvarez Belón family. María and Enrique Álvarez Belón, along with their sons Lucas, Simón, and Tomás, traveled from their home in Japan for a relaxing vacation at a Thai beach resort.

Two days into the vacation, the ocean rose without warning and devastated Thailand's western coast. The tsunami killed an estimated 228,000 people across 15 countries.[1] The Álvarez Belón family was one of thousands of families who struggled to survive in the

Some scenes of *The Impossible* were filmed at a resort in Khao Lak, Thailand. This is where the Álvarez Belón family was staying when the 2004 tsunami hit. >>

In one scene of *The Impossible*, Tom's Lucas and Naomi Watts's Maria cling to a fallen tree trunk to stay afloat as water churns around them.

tsunami's aftermath. When massive waves hit the resort, the family was separated. *The Impossible* shows how they fought against impossible odds to survive and find one another again.

For the film, Bayona changed the Álvarez Belón family's name to Bennett. He also changed some of the family members' first names. Bayona cast Naomi Watts and Ewan McGregor as married couple Maria and Henry Bennett. He needed a young actor to play Lucas, the oldest of the couple's three sons. Bayona watched a video of Tom talking about *Billy Elliot* on YouTube and was impressed. He invited Tom to audition for the role.

After several auditions, Tom landed the role of 12-year-old Lucas. He heard the news while with his family at a sporting event. Tom celebrated by running around the field. However, once his initial excitement faded, Tom panicked. He had never worked on a movie before. He would be filming scenes with established, experienced actors such as Watts and McGregor. Tom felt a little nervous.

PREPARING FOR THE ROLE

Tom's fears, however, were unfounded. Both McGregor and Watts welcomed the young actor with open arms. The cast spent a month in rehearsals before filming. This gave Tom and Watts time to bond and build a relationship, which strengthened their portrayal of a mother and son on-screen.

Tom credited Watts with helping him through the entire moviemaking process. "From the first moment I met Naomi, I knew I was in safe hands and that I'd be looked after and she'd really guide me throughout the film," Tom said. "I have learned so much from her. She's so generous with her acting, even if she's not on camera, she'll give it her best to help you. It's been the best thing for me, ever."[2]

A YOUNG TALENT

In a 2012 interview, director J. A. Bayona spoke about the process of filming *The Impossible*. He shared his thoughts about working with Tom Holland in the film, describing the child actor as disciplined and responsible on set. Bayona was also impressed with Tom's acting abilities. "He was able to get into the moment, and every time that I said cut, he was playing again with the other kid actors," Bayona said. "[Tom] is able to work as a professional actor. But at the same time, he is a 13-year-old boy, and he is able to keep the innocence of a kid, and that played a major role in his performance."[4]

Tom also prepared for the role by meeting with the real-life Lucas. Over the course of several meetings, Lucas described his experience in Thailand to Tom. "He spoke about the feelings and the emotions he was going through, throughout his experience, and as an actor, that is so helpful because he is the person that understands this story most. To have him there to answer your questions, to give you advice, to give you different sort of ideas about a scene is really, really helpful," explained Tom.[3]

FILMING CHALLENGES

Filming for *The Impossible* lasted several months. Some scenes were filmed on location in Thailand, while others were filmed in Spain. Tom faced several challenges during the filming process. First, he had to get used to

Director J. A. Bayona, *left*, insisted on using practical effects to make the tsunami scenes in *The Impossible* more realistic. This required Tom and Watts to spend hours shooting scenes in the water.

the differences between performing onstage for a live audience and performing in front of cameras.

Performing onstage required emphasizing emotions so faraway audience members could see them. But cameras could get much closer to actors. This required actors to tone down their emotions to make them more realistic.

Additionally, Tom's scenes were often physically demanding. The movie's water scenes were filmed in Spain in a 35,000-gallon (132,490 L) water tank about the size of a soccer field.[5] Human-made waves churned the water to simulate the moment when the tsunami hit.

"When we were filming that whole tsunami sequence, it was terrifying," Tom said. "People think that the film was shot using green screen over a short period of time, but the minimum of green screen effects were used. We were in that tank for six weeks. It was very real. You can imagine how tiring and brutal that was."[6]

Playing Lucas was also emotionally draining for Tom. In the film, Maria and Lucas are separated from the rest of their family after the tsunami hits. With Maria seriously injured, the responsibility of getting help for her falls on Lucas's shoulders. Filming the scenes in which Lucas watches his mother suffer was especially difficult for Tom. The young actor remembered doing one difficult take several times in a row and going home feeling exhausted.

BOX OFFICE HIT

The Impossible was first released in Spain in October 2012. In January 2013, the movie hit theaters in the United States. The film was a box office success, earning nearly $200 million worldwide.[7] Critics praised the film, its director, and its actors. In one review, *Variety* film critic Justin Chang wrote, "Holland, in his live-action big-screen debut, is wonderful as a kind, somewhat short-tempered kid who still has plenty to learn."[8]

Tom won the Young British Performer of the Year award at the 2013 London Critics' Circle Film Awards. The awards ceremony took place at a hotel in London.

Watts's performance as Maria earned her several award nominations. She was nominated for the Academy Award for Best Actress and the Golden Globe Award for Best Performance by an Actress in a Motion Picture—Drama. Tom was also nominated for some awards. He won several, including the London Critics' Circle Film Award for Young British Performer of the Year. Tom's breakout performance in *The Impossible* established him as a rising star.

BACK TO SCHOOL

In between filming *The Impossible* in 2010 and its release in 2012, Tom returned to school at Wimbledon College. This is a secondary school in London for boys ages 11 to 18. In 2012, Tom completed his General Certificate of Secondary Education (GCSE) exams. In the United Kingdom, students usually take GCSE exams between the ages of 14 and 16. The exams test students' mastery of several subjects and can be used to determine their future educational paths.

After finishing his exams, 16-year-old Tom enrolled in a two-year program at the BRIT School for Performing Arts and Technology, where he studied theater and media. Tom admitted that his early success on the stage and screen added pressure to school, especially in drama class. He said, "I remember stepping up on stage and someone

BRIT SCHOOL

The BRIT School for Performing Arts and Technology, located in Croydon, South London, is a free, government-funded institution for students ages 14 to 19. Established in 1991, it offers specialized education in music, theater, dance, film, digital design, and visual arts. The BRIT School is famous for the practical, performance-led approach it uses to train students for creative arts careers.
The school emphasizes creativity, collaboration, and industry engagement. Tom Holland, Adele, Amy Winehouse, and FKA twigs are among the school's famous alumni.

saying, 'Oh, here he is, Billy Elliot, this should be good' and I was like, oh god, what if it's not good and I completely ruin it and look like an idiot. So there is a level of pressure on me to perform well."[9] Still, Tom appreciated the opportunity to learn more about acting at the BRIT School. Instead of learning onstage or on a movie set, the actor now had time to study performance techniques in more detail.

> **"I always knew that I wanted to have a future in the performing arts. I had no idea that it was going to be acting in movies."[10]**
>
> **—Holland, 2012**

NEW PROJECTS

While attending the BRIT School, Tom read scripts, auditioned, and looked for his next projects. In 2013, he landed the role of Isaac in *How I Live Now*. This film follows an American girl named Daisy, played by Saoirse Ronan, who travels to England and fights to survive as World War III breaks out.

Tom enjoyed working on the film. But he also felt that playing Isaac, who was similar to himself in real life, was not challenging enough. What Tom loved most about acting was the ability to play a completely different character who was going through new experiences.

In 2015, Holland attended the New York City premiere of *In the Heart of the Sea* along with costars Benjamin Walker and Chris Hemsworth and director Ron Howard, *left to right*.

In September 2013, Tom began working on *In the Heart of the Sea*. The film, directed by Ron Howard, is a historical adventure story set in the early 1800s. It is based on the book *In the Heart of the Sea: The Tragedy of the Whaleship* Essex. The *Essex* was a real American whaling ship that sank after being rammed by a whale in 1820. This tragedy is said to have inspired the classic 1851 novel *Moby Dick*. The movie stars Chris Hemsworth as the *Essex*'s first mate. Tom plays the ship's cabin boy, Thomas Nickerson.

Filming took place in the Canary Islands, which are located off Africa's northwestern coast, and on sets in

Leavesden, England. Tom and the other actors ate a restrictive diet to lose weight so they would look like their starving characters. While filming, they spent hours soaking wet. In one intense scene, Tom's character has to climb into the belly of a dead whale to get its oil.

WOLF HALL

In 2015, Tom accepted a role in a BBC television series called *Wolf Hall*. Based on a best-selling book series, this historical drama takes place during the Tudor period of 1485 to 1603, during which the Tudor family ruled England. The show follows Englishman Thomas Cromwell's rise to power in King Henry VIII's court. Tom plays the role of Cromwell's son, Gregory Cromwell, in several episodes of the show.

"Ron was adamant on making everything as authentic as possible," Tom said. "He had a prosthetic whale head built, and I had to cover myself in Vaseline and clamber in. . . . The worst part was trying to get back out again because it was so slippy. I'd get halfway up and slip right back in again. Eventually, they'd throw me a rope and drag me out. It was like being born, over and over again, all night long."[11]

In the Heart of the Sea premiered in December 2015. It was unable to earn back its $100 million budget, bringing in only $94 million.[12] Critics said the film did not appeal to Hemsworth's main fan base. Despite the film's reception, Tom was about to land the biggest role of his career.

CHAPTER FOUR

BECOMING SPIDER-MAN

In 2014, *The Amazing Spider-Man 2* hit theaters. It starred Andrew Garfield as the famous web-slinging superhero. After the film failed to meet expectations at the box office, plans for a third installment were scrapped by Sony Pictures Entertainment, which owns the film rights to Spider-Man.

Soon after, Kevin Feige and Ike Perlmutter from Marvel Studios asked Sony for permission to use the Spider-Man character in one of their upcoming movies, *Captain America: Civil War.* Feige and Perlmutter also wanted Sony to let them coproduce the next *Spider-Man* movie. The Sony executives were hesitant, but eventually a deal was reached.

Captain America: Civil War **features a battle at an airport, during which Holland's Spider-Man steals Captain America's shield.** >>

In February 2015, Sony and Marvel Studios announced that Spider-Man would appear in a Marvel movie in 2016. The film was later revealed to be *Captain America: Civil War.* The character would also star in a stand-alone movie produced by Marvel Studios and released by Sony in 2017.

Anthony and Joe Russo, the directors of *Captain America: Civil War,* were relieved that the two studios had come to an agreement to include Spider-Man in their movie. They had spent months developing their vision for the character in the film. It would have been extremely difficult to take him out of the story so late in the production process.

The Russos were also excited to bring Spider-Man into the Marvel Cinematic Universe (MCU). In an interview,

MARVEL CINEMATIC UNIVERSE

The Marvel Cinematic Universe (MCU) is an interconnected film and television franchise based on characters from Marvel Comics and produced by Marvel Studios. All MCU stories take place in the same shared universe, allowing characters and plotlines to cross over between movies and TV shows. The MCU began in 2008 with the film *Iron Man*, starring Robert Downey Jr. The universe includes popular superheroes such as Thor, Captain America, Black Widow, Doctor Strange, the Hulk, and Black Panther. The MCU has stand-alone movies for many of its heroes as well as ensemble movies that feature several heroes working together.

the Russos explained that they liked Spider-Man because "he's a high schooler with this power and responsibility, and it makes him very distinct as a hero. It makes him distinct from the other characters in the Marvel Universe, who are confident, experienced superheroes."[1]

"To be in a movie of that scale with actors of that caliber was really a dream come true, and also an eye opener to the responsibility I've been given."[2]

—Holland on playing Spider-Man in *Captain America: Civil War*, 2017

A few months later, in June 2015, Marvel Studios announced that it had found its new Peter Parker, 19-year-old Tom Holland. At the time, Holland was mostly unknown to American audiences. He had experience acting in a few films and onstage, but joining the MCU as a beloved superhero opened the door to a new level of fame.

After Holland's casting was announced, curious fans noted that he was younger than previous actors who had played Spider-Man. Feige explained that the studio wanted a young-looking actor for Spider-Man. "We want to play with Spider-Man in the high school years because frankly, there've been five Spider-Man films, and . . . there are so many things from the comics that haven't been done yet," Feige said. "The most obvious being the 'young, doesn't quite fit in' kid before his powers, and

Holland attended the 2016 London premiere of *Captain America: Civil War*. He interacted with fans and signed autographs.

then the fella that puts on a mask and swings around and fights bad guys and doesn't shut up, which is something we want to play with."[3]

ON SET WITH CAPTAIN AMERICA

Once Holland's casting was announced, Marvel immediately put the young actor to work. A few days later, Holland was on the set of *Captain America: Civil War*. The movie stars Chris Evans as Captain America and Robert Downey Jr. as Iron Man. In the film, the government decides to support a law that puts limitations on superheroes, sparking a disagreement among the superhero team known as the Avengers. This leads to a civil war in which Iron Man and his allies, including Black Panther, Vision, Black Widow, and War Machine, fight Captain America and his allies, including Bucky Barnes, Falcon, Scarlet Witch, Hawkeye, and Ant-Man. Holland's Spider-Man joins the fight on Iron Man's side.

HIGH-TECH SUPER SUIT

Before Peter Parker meets Tony Stark, also known as Iron Man, his Spider-Man suit is very simple. It consists of a mask, a red hoodie with a spider symbol, goggles, and blue long johns. Stark creates a high-tech, custom version of the suit for Peter, which the young superhero wears for the first time during *Captain America: Civil War.* The now iconic red-and-blue Spider-Man suit, known as the "Stark Suit," has several unique features. These include mechanical eyes that can display information to the wearer, retractable web wings, upgraded web-shooters, and a built-in GPS tracker.

Holland spent about a week filming his scenes for *Captain America: Civil War.* After filming, he returned home. He didn't hear anything from Marvel, which made him nervous. "I was convinced they were going to fire me. I don't know why," Holland said. "*Civil War* hadn't come out yet, and I just didn't hear anything from anyone. I can't really explain it. It was awful, but they didn't [fire me]—obviously."[4]

Captain America: Civil War hit theaters in May 2016. It was a massive success, earning $1.15 billion at the worldwide box office.[5] Audiences were thrilled with

Holland's performance as the new Spider-Man and with his entrance into the MCU.

"In what's already one of Marvel Studios's best movies, Spider-Man stands out. Holland manages to steal the show in what amounts to an extended cameo by capturing the bright-eyed, youthful wit that has resonated with fans since the character's creation," wrote film critic Kwame Opam for the website the *Verge*. "Any die-hard fan worried about this being the third take on Spidey in 15 years should know that Tom Holland is arguably the best onscreen Spider-Man to date," Opam added.[6]

THE LOST CITY OF Z

Before Holland donned his Spider-Man suit again, he headed to Ireland and Colombia in the fall of 2015 to film another action-adventure movie, *The Lost City of Z*. The film is based on a best-selling book by author David Grann. It tells the story of real-life explorer Percy Fawcett, who disappeared on a 1920s expedition to find a mythical city in the Amazon jungle. The film stars Charlie Hunnam as Fawcett, along with Robert Pattinson and Sienna Miller. Holland plays Fawcett's eldest son, Jack.

On the last day of filming in Colombia, the film's director, James Gray, saw a few videos of Holland doing

In *The Lost City of Z,* Holland's character, Jack Fawcett, is 21 years old when he accompanies his father on an Amazonian expedition.

In one scene of *The Lost City of Z*, Percy and Jack encounter Indigenous people while trekking through the Amazon jungle. The real-life Percy and Jack disappeared in the Amazon in 1925.

flips on a beach. Gray jokingly challenged the actor to prove it was not a fake video. Holland accepted the challenge but forgot he was still wearing the heavy boots that were part of his character's costume.

"I had these stupid leather boots on, I tried to do a backflip, and [I] just broke my face," Holland said. "I mean, I've been a gymnast since I was a little kid. It's been years since I haven't really landed one, and I remember hitting my face on the floor and going . . . 'That didn't happen.' I stood up, I thought I knocked my teeth out, and the makeup artist was laughing at me. And when she saw my face, it went from 'Haha' to *'Oh, medic, medic!'*"[7]

As blood poured down Holland's face, the on-set medic temporarily set the actor's broken nose.

The makeup artist reapplied the fake mustache that Holland wore in the film, and he finished filming his last scene. Back home in England, he got his nose fixed. It was a little awkward when Holland had to tell Marvel that their new Spider-Man had a broken nose. Holland gave them a shortened version of the events.

The Lost City of Z hit theaters in 2017 and received favorable reviews from critics. Some viewers, however, thought the movie dragged and was uneven in parts. Despite receiving mostly positive reviews, the film flopped at the box office. It made under $20 million, less than its production budget of $30 million.[8] Up until this point, Holland had played supporting roles in his movies. Now it was time for him to step into the lead role as Spider-Man.

HINTS FOR A NEW *SPIDER-MAN* MOVIE

In *Captain America: Civil War,* the Russo brothers included several hints about Holland's upcoming *Spider-Man* stand-alone movie. *Civil War* includes a few short scenes set in Queens, New York, that show Peter Parker living with his Aunt May and trying to figure out his superpowers. In the film's closing credits, another scene shows Peter trying to explain to Aunt May how he got his injuries and discovering a gadget that Tony Stark made for him.

CHAPTER FIVE

SWINGING TO STARDOM

Captain America: Civil War introduced Holland's Spider-Man to audiences worldwide. Soon it was time for the young actor to tackle his biggest project yet: starring in a stand-alone *Spider-Man* movie. But first, the actor had to go back to school.

The script for the new *Spider-Man* movie focused on Peter Parker as a high school student. The 15-year-old tech whiz attends the fictional Midtown School of Science and Technology in New York City. Growing up in England and attending an all-boys prep school, Holland had a very different school experience than most American students. So executives at Marvel Studios came up with a plan to help Holland

The *Spider-Man: Homecoming* crew not only had Holland go undercover as a high school student but also used several real high schools as filming locations. >>

Bronx Science is famous for its green doors and large mosaic mural, which can be seen from outside through the school's front windows. Holland went undercover at the school for three days.

research his role before filming began. The actor would go undercover at a real New York City high school.

Marvel executives chose the Bronx High School of Science, also known as Bronx Science. It is one of the top high schools in the United States. To attend, students must pass a competitive exam. It was the closest real-life school to Peter Parker's fictional high school. Marvel decided to have Holland shadow a real student at the school who was studying subjects that Peter Parker would study, such as science, technology, engineering, and math.

After talking with school administrators, Marvel found a student for Holland to shadow. Senior Arun Bishop was not only taking advanced science and math classes but was also the captain of the school's robotics team. Bishop was talking to a school adviser when the school's vice principal came up to him and told him about Marvel's idea. Bishop, a big Marvel fan, agreed to the plan.

WHO IS BEN PERKINS?

When Holland went undercover as a student at the Bronx High School of Science, he had a fake name picked out. But when he went into the school and someone asked what his name was, Holland panicked and forgot it. He said the first name that came to mind: Ben Perkins. Ben Perkins was Holland's real-life acting coach, who was with the actor in New York City at the time. Although Holland had not planned on using Ben Perkins as his undercover name, he decided to roll with it.

On an early morning in February 2016, Holland met Bishop outside Bronx Science. The two teens talked and went over Holland's undercover story. Only Bishop and a few teachers and administrators knew who Holland really was.

To everyone else at the school, Holland would be introduced as Bishop's cousin, Ben. Holland would use an American accent. If anyone asked about the new kid, they would say that Holland's dad was in the military and had just been stationed near New York.

When it was time for school to start, Holland followed Bishop into Bronx Science, carrying a backpack like the other students. Holland shadowed Bishop through his daily schedule. The actor went to physics, linear algebra, and calculus classes. Holland enjoyed pretending to be an American high schooler. In turn, Bishop found Holland easy to talk to and thought he was just like any other teen.

On his second day at Bronx Science, Holland's excitement began to wane. Like many teens, he started to get a little bored in class. To amuse himself, Holland began trying to convince some of the other students that he was Spider-Man. "Most of them wouldn't believe him at all. Because that just doesn't make sense, right?" Bishop said. "Why, at Bronx Science, would there be an actor who's been shadowing me for a day and a half?"[1]

For fun, Holland and Bishop began interviewing students during their lunch period. They asked them questions about Marvel movies and the new Spider-Man. Still, no one recognized Holland.

"No one knew. I actually have videos on my phone of me interviewing people and asking them what they thought of the new Spider-Man in *Civil War*," Holland said. "They were like, 'Oh, he's great, I love him,' and then some people were like, 'Nah, I don't love him, he's not great'—and I was standing right in front of them! . . . It was really fun."[2]

SPIDER-MAN: HOMECOMING

Filming for *Spider-Man: Homecoming* began in June 2016. Most of the movie was filmed at Pinewood Atlanta Studios in Georgia. Filming also took place in Los Angeles, California; New York City; and Berlin, Germany. In addition to Holland, the film stars Robert Downey Jr. as Iron Man, Marisa Tomei as Aunt May, and Michael Keaton as Adrian Toomes, or the Vulture. Teen actors Zendaya and Jacob Batalon play Peter's friends, MJ and Ned.

Spider-Man: Homecoming follows Peter Parker after he returns home from his experience with the Avengers in *Captain America: Civil War*. He attempts to balance his life as a normal teenager with his alternate identity as Spider-Man. Peter lives with his Aunt May and has Iron Man as a mentor. But he finds himself put to the test

MOVIE NIGHT

Spider-Man: Homecoming is a coming-of-age film, or one that focuses on a character's transition from youth to adulthood. Director Jon Watts wanted the cast, especially Holland and the other lead actors, to understand the genre. So he gave them a homework assignment. He asked them to watch several famous coming-of-age movies from the 1980s, including *The Breakfast Club*, *Ferris Bueller's Day Off*, and *Pretty in Pink*. Holland and his costars gathered at his house in Atlanta, where they ordered pizza and binge-watched all the movies in one day.

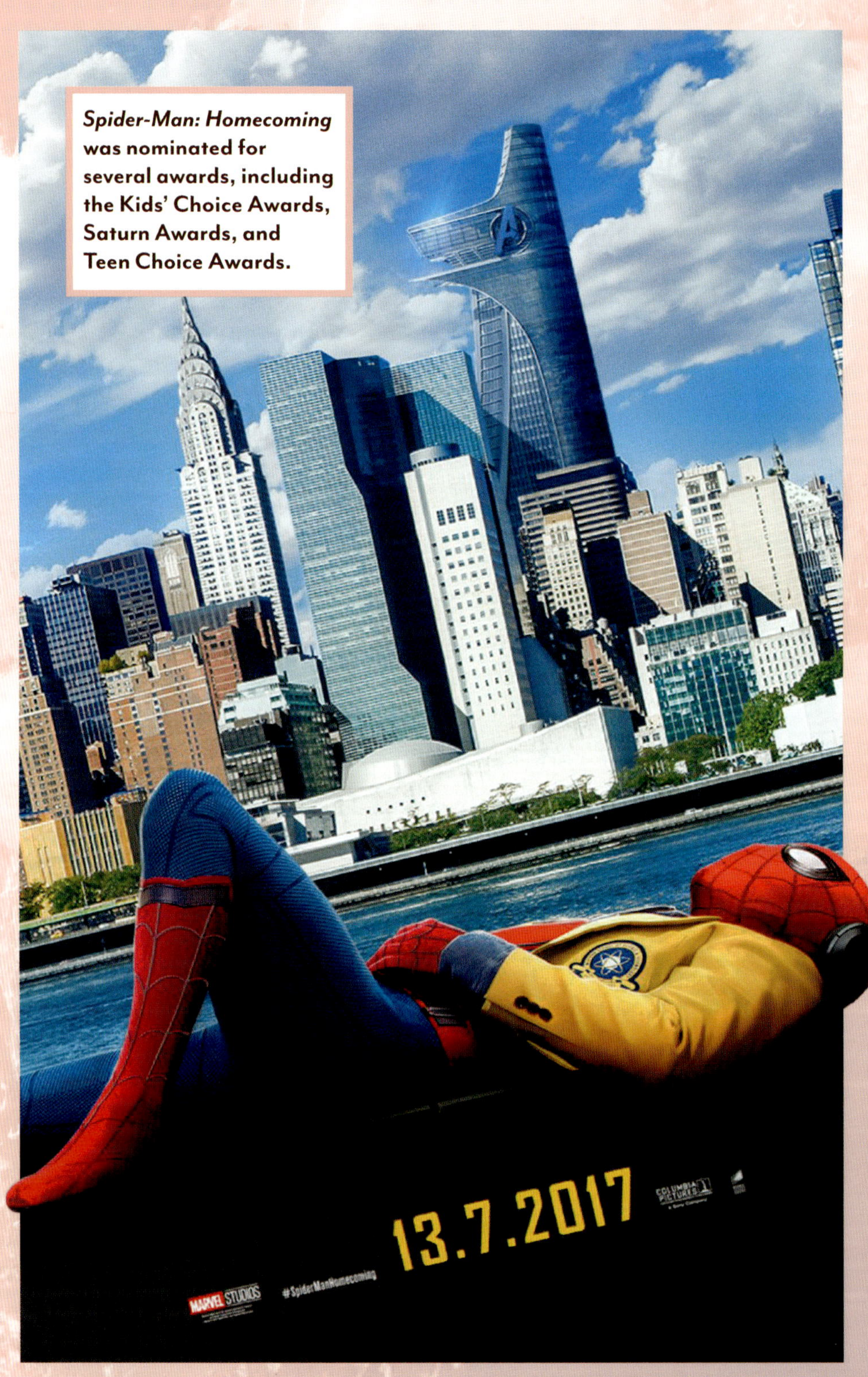

Spider-Man: Homecoming was nominated for several awards, including the Kids' Choice Awards, Saturn Awards, and Teen Choice Awards.

when a new villain, the Vulture, threatens everything and everyone he holds dear.

Holland remembers *Homecoming* as the first time he really put on Spider-Man's iconic suit. On the set of *Civil War*, Holland had joined the cast so late that there was no time to make him a custom suit. Scenes had already been filmed with Holland's stunt double, so the filmmakers decided to alter the stunt double's suit to fit Holland.

"My stunt double was a good two or three inches taller than me and stockier than me, so the first time I ever tried [the suit] on it was kind of like a saggy, sad Spider-Man," Holland recalled.[3] But for *Homecoming*, the experience was much different.

"The time I tried it on for real and it fit perfectly was one of the most surreal experiences of my life," he said. "It's been my dream since I was a kid, and the fact that it was coming true before my own eyes was such a crazy feeling. I was just so proud of myself and delighted with how my career had gone and where I was standing."[4]

PERFORMING STUNTS

Holland's acrobatic background helped him perform several stunts in *Homecoming*. In one scene, Spider-Man climbs the Washington Monument to save his friends.

The production team built a replica of the monument's sections on an Atlanta soundstage. The replica's side was built at an angle.

Holland climbed up the side supported by safety cables, and the filmmakers used camera angles to make it look as if he were climbing the vertical monument. Another replica re-created the monument's top and sides. Wearing safety cables and a harness, Holland climbed, leaped, jumped, and flipped on the replica.

For actions that were too dangerous to perform as real-life stunts, Holland wore a motion-capture suit that recorded his movements while he was safely on the ground. The production team took the motion-capture footage and used computer graphics (CG) to create what audiences would see on-screen. Using motion-capture footage from Holland's movements made the CG appear more realistic in the film.

PUTTING ON THE SUIT

Putting on Spider-Man's suit can be a complicated process. Holland explained that the amount of time he needs to get dressed in the costume depends on the scene and the type of suit needed. For scenes that require wearing a harness underneath the suit, it takes about 45 minutes to get ready. If Holland is wearing the suit without a harness, it takes about 25 minutes.[5] Because it takes so long to get in and out of the suit, Holland says he plans his bathroom breaks carefully on set.

Holland worked with a team of stunt coordinators to pull off the Washington Monument elevator scene in *Homecoming*.

Later in the movie, Spider-Man shoots his webs to stop an elevator from hurtling down an elevator shaft. Pulling back, he braces his legs on either side of the elevator opening. Eventually, he is pulled headfirst into the shaft.

To film the scene, Holland sat with his legs braced against an elevator opening and then dived headfirst off a ledge while connected to wires. Holland initially hesitated to do the stunt himself, especially since he had just eaten.

The stunt required him to wear a tight corset harness, and he worried it might make him vomit. However, Holland was able to perform the stunt successfully.

ROMANCE BLOSSOMS

The *Spider-Man* films have a history of romantic chemistry between the lead actors spilling from the big screen into real life. The first Spider-Man, Tobey Maguire, dated costar Kirsten Dunst after they met on the set of the 2002 film *Spider-Man*. Dunst plays Spider-Man's love interest, Mary Jane, in the movie.

The second Spider-Man, Andrew Garfield, also dated his on-screen girlfriend, Emma Stone. She plays Gwen Stacy, Spider-Man's crush, in the second Spider-Man film franchise. When producer Amy Pascal first cast Holland and Zendaya in *Homecoming*, she warned them against getting romantically involved with each other.

"I gave the same advice to Andrew and Emma. It can just complicate things, you know? And they all ignored me," Pascal said.[6]

Holland and Zendaya worked closely together on the set of *Homecoming*. At first, the young actors' on-screen chemistry developed into a close off-screen friendship. The costars frequently appeared together during the

Holland and his *Homecoming* costar Zendaya appeared together at a 2017 promotional event in Madrid, Spain.

Homecoming press tour, at various publicity events, and on social media. Rumors soon began to swirl about a potential romantic relationship between Holland and Zendaya. However, the two insisted they were just friends.

SURPASSING EXPECTATIONS

By late 2016, anticipation for *Spider-Man: Homecoming* was growing. The first trailer came out in December 2016. As the film's July release date approached, social media buzz increased. *Homecoming* became the most talked-about movie on social media. Executives at Marvel and Sony tried to set moderate expectations, estimating that the film would bring in about $80 million at the domestic box office during its opening weekend.[7]

Homecoming hit theaters on July 7, 2017. It surpassed expectations, bringing in an estimated

Holland won the EE Rising Star Award at the 2017 BAFTA Awards ceremony. The British public votes to select the winner of the category.

$117 million at the domestic box office in its first weekend. “Everyone at Sony and Marvel are thrilled,” said Sony marketing executive Josh Greenstein. “It’s safe to say it’s a triumphant return for Spider-Man.”[8] The movie went on to earn $881 million at the worldwide box office, well beyond its budget of $175 million.[9]

The film received mostly positive reviews. Film critic Benjamin Lee wrote, “*Spider-Man: Homecoming* is so joyously entertaining that it’s enough to temporarily cure any superhero fatigue. There’s wit, smarts, and a nifty, inventive plot that serves as a reminder of what buoyant fun such films can bring. It might have taken three attempts, but Spider-Man has finally spun gold.” Lee also praised Holland’s portrayal of Peter Parker. “Holland is sensational: funny, awkward, and believably vulnerable, adding a necessary tension to his early attempts at superheroics,” wrote Lee.[10]

Holland received several nominations and awards for his portrayal of Peter Parker in *Civil War* and *Homecoming*. He won a Saturn Award for Best Performance by a Younger Actor and a Teen Choice Award for Choice Summer Movie Actor. In 2017, Holland was also awarded the EE Rising Star Award at the BAFTA Awards. Holland’s Spider-Man was officially a hit.

CHAPTER SIX

MORE SPIDER-MAN

A few months after filming *Homecoming*, Holland put his Spider-Man suit on once again. This time, he joined an ensemble cast of Avengers superheroes for two movies, *Avengers: Infinity War* and *Avengers: Endgame*. The movies were filmed back-to-back beginning in January 2017.

Anthony and Joe Russo directed the two new films. The first, *Avengers: Infinity War*, pits the Avengers against the powerful warlord Thanos, who is trying to collect all six Infinity Stones. Each stone controls an essential part of existence: time, space, reality, mind, power, and soul. Whoever holds all the Infinity Stones will have immense power.

When Peter Parker first appears in *Avengers: Infinity War*, he sneaks off a school bus in order to swing into action as Spider-Man. >>

TTUCE
TASTE OF

THE AVENGERS

In the MCU, the Avengers are a group of superheroes who work together to protect the world. The character Nick Fury came up with the idea of the Avengers. He is the director of the Strategic Homeland Intervention, Enforcement, and Logistics Division (S.H.I.E.L.D.), an intelligence agency that works to maintain national and global security. The original group of heroes included Iron Man, Black Widow, Captain America, Hawkeye, Thor, and the Hulk. The group operates independently of any government agency. The wealthy Tony Stark provides them with equipment and resources.

Thanos plans to use the stones to erase half of all life in the universe. The Avengers, including Spider-Man, join forces to stop Thanos from achieving his goal. However, the film has a shocking ending. Thanos gathers the six stones and snaps his fingers, causing half of all living things to disintegrate into dust. Several Avengers are among the victims.

Holland felt a little starstruck while filming *Infinity War* alongside so many well-known actors. "To be 21 and to get the chance to work with people like this is amazing," he said. "It was just a real whirlwind to walk on set and see 30 of your favorite actors dressed up like superheroes, just having a coffee and hanging out. It was so bizarre!"[1]

The film's production was kept top secret to prevent any spoilers from leaking before the movie's release. Cast members were instructed to turn in their script pages each day before leaving the set. When Holland realized he

***Infinity War*'s tragic ending saw beloved characters such as Spider-Man, Doctor Strange, Scarlet Witch, and Black Panther disintegrate into dust, shocking audiences.**

had mistakenly taken his script pages home one day, he decided to burn them and posted a video of it on Instagram as proof.

Holland and most of his costars were not given the entire script. They knew little about the movie besides their scenes. In one interview, Holland joked about his inability to keep secrets and said that he didn't know anything about the film's plot.

Infinity War hit theaters in April 2018 and became a massive box office success. The film earned more than $2 billion at the worldwide box office.[2] Critics praised the film for its visual effects and thrilling action sequences. It was nominated for several awards, including the Academy Award for Best Visual Effects.

One of the movie's most emotional scenes happens at the end, when Holland's Spider-Man becomes one of Thanos's victims and disintegrates in Iron Man's arms. Holland later spoke about filming his character's death scene. "People tell me they imagine that scene must have been horrendous to shoot, but I look back on it with nothing but happiness," he said. "It was amazing. I loved it. I got to hug Robert Downey Jr., like, 60 times, and cry on his shoulder. What's not to love?"[3]

AVENGERS: ENDGAME

The storyline of *Avengers: Endgame* picks up where *Infinity War* ends. The surviving Avengers regroup and devise a plan to travel back in time to collect the Infinity Stones before Thanos does. They hope that if they succeed, they will be able to restore everyone who disintegrated at the end of *Infinity War*. The journey through time takes the Avengers back to key moments from their past films. However, Thanos discovers the team's plan and launches a massive attack against them. The Avengers who disappeared in *Infinity War*, including Holland's Spider-Man, return just in time to join the final battle against Thanos and his army.

Once again, details about the movie's plot were tightly guarded. By the time *Endgame* was in production, Holland had developed a reputation for being unable to keep secrets. Directors Joe and Anthony Russo joked that they would not give the young actor much information because they feared he would accidentally reveal important details or plot points in press interviews. While filming some scenes, the Russos didn't even tell Holland whom his character was supposed to be fighting.

LEARNING AN AMERICAN ACCENT

To play Peter Parker, who is a native New Yorker, Holland had to speak with an American accent. He worked with a dialect coach to master how an American teen talked. Holland sometimes had difficulty maintaining the accent when improvising lines. When improvising, he focused more on what he was saying rather than on how he was saying it. Holland also explains that he tends to imitate and talk like the people with whom he works. This means he must stay focused while filming to ensure Peter Parker sounds like a kid from Queens.

One of the most climactic moments in *Endgame* occurs in the final battle, which pits the Avengers and their allies against Thanos and his army. Captain America, played by Chris Evans, stands with the Avengers and leads the charge into battle with the line "Avengers, assemble!" The scene had to be refilmed after Holland started moving too early because he didn't hear Evans say the line.

"I just went 'Arrrghhh!'—I ran off by myself," Holland said. "I got like 30 feet and I had to turn around and . . . walk back to [all] my childhood heroes and be like, 'Sorry guys, I got that wrong.'"[4]

Endgame arrived in theaters in April 2019. It shattered box office records, earning more than $1.2 billion at the worldwide box office in only five days. It was the fastest film in history to surpass $1 billion,

In 2018, Holland and Zendaya were spotted in New York City filming a stunt scene for *Far from Home*.

breaking the previous 11-day record set in 2018 by *Infinity War.*[5] In total, the film grossed, or earned, nearly $2.8 billion at the worldwide box office, making it the second-highest-grossing film of all time.[6]

FAR FROM HOME

While working on the *Avengers* movies, Holland was also preparing for his second solo *Spider-Man* film. One day after the first *Homecoming* trailer came out in December 2016, Sony had officially announced a *Spider-Man* sequel tentatively scheduled for a July 2019 release. This release timing set up a careful balancing act with Marvel's *Avengers: Endgame*, scheduled to come out in April 2019, to prevent any *Endgame* spoilers from leaking.

In June 2018, Holland accidentally revealed the sequel's title before filming began. In a video posted to his Instagram account, Holland held up a tablet that revealed *Spider-Man: Far from Home* as the film's working title. He acknowledged that his Spider-Man character had died at the end of *Avengers: Infinity War*, which left fans with a lot of unanswered questions about how everything would work out for Peter Parker.

Filming for *Far from Home* began in July 2018. It was primarily filmed in several locations in Europe, including

England, Italy, Spain, and the Czech Republic. Actor Jake Gyllenhaal joined the cast as Quentin Beck, who is later revealed to be the villain Mysterio. Samuel L. Jackson also appears in his recurring MCU role of Nick Fury, the founder of the Avengers.

For Holland, returning to the character of Spider-Man felt comfortable. It was his second *Spider-Man* movie and marked the fifth time he'd played the superhero on-screen. The actor felt like he knew the character pretty well by that point. Holland also pointed out that most of the people who had worked on *Spider-Man: Homecoming* had returned for *Far from Home*, including director Jon Watts. To Holland, the set felt like a reunion.

The storyline for *Far from Home* starts after the events of *Avengers: Endgame*, on the last day of school before summer break. Peter Parker and his friends embark on a summer trip to Europe. Peter looks forward to taking a break from his Spider-Man responsibilities.

But Peter's vacation plans are dashed when Nick Fury arrives and enlists the young superhero to help unravel the mystery of strange creature attacks occurring across Europe. Meanwhile, Peter grapples with his feelings for MJ, once again played by Zendaya, and the pair begins a romantic relationship.

To prepare for the film's stunts, Holland trained for several weeks with stunt coordinator George Cottle. One of the most challenging stunts was a scene in which Peter and MJ swing on one of Peter's webs. To create the scene, filmmakers raised Holland and Zendaya more than 100 feet (30 m) in the air with wires and a crane.[7] The two actors were dropped and swung in an arc over cardboard boxes.

For the landing and takeoff, cranes lifted the costars to different heights outside New York City's Grand Central Station and Madison Square Garden. To create midair close-up shots, filmmakers set up a large blue screen and wind fans and filmed in the parking lot of a school. The camera shots of Holland and Zendaya were combined with CG images and backgrounds to create the scenes that appeared in the movie.

In January 2019, Sony's Columbia Pictures dropped an online teaser trailer for *Spider-Man: Far from Home*.

YOUNG FANS

One of Holland's favorite things about playing Spider-Man is meeting his littlest fans. Often, very young Spider-Man fans do not understand that Holland is an actor playing a role. Kids think he is really a superhero and ask him to do stunts and tricks. Holland plays along and talks to the kids in his Peter Parker accent. He sometimes tells them that he can't do a trick because he doesn't have his Spider-Man suit with him. But the actor does his best to keep the magic alive for the kids.

In June 2019, Holland, Jacob Batalon, *center*, and Zendaya promoted *Far from Home* at the Empire State Building in New York City. The costars participated in a special lighting ceremony.

The trailer was a sensation, getting 130 million views in its first 24 hours online. It was the biggest digital launch in Sony Pictures history, surpassing *Spider-Man: Homecoming*'s record of 116 million views in 24 hours.[8] Meanwhile, during the *Far from Home* press tour, Holland and Zendaya made many public appearances together. The costars charmed the media with their natural chemistry and playful banter, rekindling romance rumors.

Far from Home hit theaters on July 2, 2019. It became the first *Spider-Man* movie to earn more than $1 billion at the worldwide box office, pulling in $1.13 billion.[9] It took the top spot as Sony Pictures' highest-grossing film. The movie received mostly positive reviews from audiences and critics.

Far from Home was also nominated for several awards, including the Critics Choice Award for Best Action Movie. Holland won several awards for his performance in the film. These included a Saturn Award for Best Performance by a Younger Actor and a People's Choice Award for Favorite Action Movie Star.

CHAPTER SEVEN

BEYOND THE WEB

After swinging to fame as Spider-Man, Holland explored several darker, more serious film roles. These roles were very different than the characters he had previously played. They allowed the young actor to showcase his range and demonstrate that he was more than just a friendly neighborhood Spider-Man.

In February 2019, Holland traveled to Alabama to film *The Devil All the Time*, a psychological crime thriller produced for the Netflix streaming service. Directed by Antonio Campos, the film is based on a book by Donald Ray Pollock. It follows several characters whose lives intersect between World War II (1939–1945) and the 1960s. Holland plays Arvin Russell, a young man

Holland's character, Arvin Russell, is the central figure of *The Devil All the Time.* Arvin is a young man who had a troubled childhood. >>

attempting to do what he thinks is right even if it takes him down a path of violence and revenge. The role required the British actor to master a southern American accent. Holland joined an ensemble cast that included Robert Pattinson, Bill Skarsgård, Sebastian Stan, Riley Keough, Haley Bennett, Mia Wasikowska, and Jason Clarke.

Holland was unsure about his ability to connect with the character of Arvin before arriving on set. "I was really nervous and scared coming on set for the first time because I didn't know if I had it in me to play this type of character," Holland said. "He is a really complicated character and it is very dark, and I had to go to places mentally that I didn't know I could go to or don't think I ever want to go to again."[1]

In the film, Arvin believes that sometimes killing is the moral and right choice. The character had a completely different mindset than any of Holland's previous characters. However, Holland trusted director Antonio Campos to guide him through the movie's dark material.

The Devil All the Time debuted on Netflix in September 2020. It was the platform's most-watched movie for its first two days.[2] Critics gave the film mixed reviews but praised the cast. Film critic Michael Phillips wrote, "It's worth seeing for an intriguingly cast ensemble. . . . Holland's terrific, taking in each new setback in Arvin's life without revealing the full extent of the damage."[3]

CHERRY

In 2019, Holland reunited with *Avengers* directors Anthony and Joe Russo. While working on *Avengers: Endgame*, the Russos approached Holland with a new project. They were making a small independent film and wanted Holland to play the lead role.

Holland accepted and signed on to the Russos' crime drama *Cherry*. The film is based on Nico Walker's 2018 novel of the same name. The book blends fictional elements with Walker's real-life experiences as a former US Army medic who later developed a drug addiction.

Holland was cast as the film's main character, Cherry. The film follows his days as a college dropout and his

In *Cherry*, Holland's character experiences the horrors of war. The Russos used special camera techniques to make the film's war scenes as realistic as possible.

NICO WALKER

The movie *Cherry* is based on the life of Nico Walker, a former US Army medic. After serving in the Iraq War (2003–2011) and experiencing severe PTSD, Walker developed an addiction to opioids and robbed several banks to buy drugs. He was arrested in 2011 and wrote *Cherry* while serving a prison sentence. The novel received critical acclaim for its raw portrayal of war, addiction, and crime. Walker used his book earnings to repay some of the banks he had robbed.

experience as an army medic in Iraq. When Cherry returns from the war, he suffers from post-traumatic stress disorder (PTSD). He develops an addiction to opioids and eventually turns to robbing banks to fund his drug use. Ciara Bravo plays Cherry's girlfriend, who later becomes his wife.

Filming began in October 2019 and lasted through mid-January 2020. Playing Cherry proved to be the most demanding role of Holland's career. The actor had to lose about 27 pounds (12 kg) because the character is emaciated due to drug addiction.[4] To lose weight, Holland exercised and ate a strict low-calorie diet.

When it got difficult, Holland remembered author Nico Walker, on whom the character of Cherry was based. "It was uncomfortable, even painful, but I do believe that if you're telling a story about a real-life person, you have a duty to do justice to them," said Holland.[5]

The film's scenes were not shot chronologically. This meant Holland had to quickly bulk up for scenes that took place earlier in the story, before Cherry's life begins to spiral out of control. Hamburgers were a staple food, helping the actor regain the weight he had lost.

While Holland did not meet with or speak to Nico Walker to prepare for the role, he felt a responsibility to play the character in a way that Walker would approve. "More than any film I have done, I have never been so nervous as at the idea of Nico watching *Cherry*," Holland said. "I hope he can be proud of what he's written, and his progression and healing, and that I've done his life justice on screen."[6]

Cherry was released in a handful of theaters in February 2021. It made its streaming debut on Apple TV+ in March 2021. The film received mixed reviews from critics and audiences. *Guardian* critic Peter Bradshaw wrote, "*Cherry* is a fervent movie, corn-fed with drama and action, but maybe a little less than the sum of its parts." He added that Holland is "a fierce, compact presence" who "certainly brings his A-game" to the film.[7]

> **"When I read a script, I ask whether I've done it before. Is it a challenge? Is this something my parents would enjoy or even my grandparents would enjoy?"[8]**
>
> **—Holland, 2021**

UNCHARTED

In 2017, Sony Pictures announced that Holland had signed on to star in its upcoming film *Uncharted*, an adaptation of the *Uncharted* video game franchise. The video game series features the character Nathan Drake, a descendant of famed explorer Sir Francis Drake. Nathan Drake is an archaeologist who travels the world searching for lost relics. For years, Sony had been working to bring the popular video game series to life on the big screen.

Sony announced that the action-adventure movie would not be a simple retelling of the stories featured in the game. Instead, the film would be a prequel. Holland would play a young Nathan Drake. Actors Mark Wahlberg and Antonio Banderas also joined the cast. After several delays, the film was ready to start production in early 2020.

In March 2020, Holland arrived in Germany for his first day of shooting on the *Uncharted* set. The COVID-19 pandemic had been steadily growing more serious in the preceding weeks, and by March, many in-person activities, projects, and events began to be canceled or delayed. Production on *Uncharted* and other projects across the entertainment industry were paused indefinitely. Schools and businesses closed as the world grappled with the outbreak. Holland returned home to London to wait out the pandemic.

Like many people worldwide, Holland spent the next few weeks and months in lockdown. During that time, he worked with his brother on writing a screenplay. He socialized with friends online. Holland also worked to help raise money for various charitable causes.

In July, filming for *Uncharted* finally resumed. In the film, Holland's Nathan Drake is a young bartender. He is recruited by veteran treasure hunter Victor "Sully" Sullivan, played by Wahlberg, to recover a treasure gathered by legendary explorer Ferdinand Magellan. The treasure was lost hundreds of years earlier. The two race around the world to locate the treasure before the evil Santiago Moncada, played by Banderas, finds it.

LIFE IN LOCKDOWN

Like many other people around the world, Holland had to adjust to life during the COVID-19 pandemic. In a virtual appearance on the talk show *Jimmy Kimmel Live* in April 2020, Holland told host Jimmy Kimmel that he was spending lockdown with his housemates in London. The actor tried to stay busy by video chatting with his movie costars and working on a screenplay for a potential future project. At the end of the virtual interview, Holland greeted Kimmel's children in character as Peter Parker.

***Uncharted* features an action-packed sequence in which Sully and Nathan struggle to stay on a cargo plane. Holland performed his own stunts for the scene.**

Filming *Uncharted* required many stunts that were tough on Holland's body. "I was going to the gym in the morning like, 'Oh, my God, I must have torn something in my leg,' and the guys were like, 'You haven't, you're just tired and you're getting older,'" Holland said.[9] In one scene, Drake falls out of a plane and struggles to climb back onboard. To perform the stunt, Holland had to be suspended by wires about 100 feet (30 m) in the air.[10]

BARTENDING SCHOOL

To prepare for his role as Nathan Drake in *Uncharted*, Holland went back to school again. This time, it was bartending school. Holland learned how to make cocktails and mix drinks. He tested his new skills at a London bar, posing undercover as a bartender for a few shifts. However, people soon began to recognize him, and word spread around London that Holland was bartending. When the bar's general manager discovered the ruse, it was the end of Holland's bartending experience.

Filming the stunt took about five weeks. "We shredded our hands to bits, and it was exhausting," Holland said. "It's a really impressive sequence, and I think that kind of level of physicality really comes through on screen, but it was . . . absolutely brutal."[11] By the time he finished filming, Holland had developed tendinitis, or inflammation of the tendons near joints. His whole body ached.

Uncharted hit theaters in February 2022, receiving mixed reviews from critics. But audiences flocked to see the movie, and it was a commercial success. The film grossed more than $407 million at the worldwide box office, with an estimated budget of $120 million.[12]

CHAPTER EIGHT

BACK TO THE BIG SCREEN

As the credits rolled at the end of *Spider-Man: Far from Home*, a scene popped up on-screen. It contained a shocking twist. In the scene, Jake Gyllenhaal's Mysterio uploads a video that plays across news outlets worldwide. In it, Mysterio blames Spider-Man for his death and publicly unmasks Peter Parker as Spider-Man.

The shocking reveal sets up the beginning of the next *Spider-Man* movie. "Now people know Peter's identity. People now think he's a villain, Mysterio plays one last trick on him and succeeds . . . [so that] means everything's different," explained Marvel Studios president Kevin Feige. "Where it goes, we'll see. But it's

In *No Way Home*, Peter's high-tech Iron Spider suit features retractable spider legs. He uses these while battling the villain Doc Ock. >>

MASK POLICY ON SET

Balancing COVID-19 protocols while filming a movie was a challenge. The *No Way Home* production crew used a light system to tell actors when to remove their masks for filming. When a blue light was lit, actors could remove their masks to film a scene. When a yellow light appeared, the cast put their masks back on and left the set. This gave crew members space to move props and perform other tasks. Once the crew finished their work and left the set, the cast could return and wait for the blue light to turn on again.

exciting that it once again sets us up for a Peter Parker story that has never been done before on film."[1]

Chris McKenna and Erik Sommers, who wrote the scripts for all three of Holland's *Spider-Man* movies, admitted that the *Far from Home* credits scene created challenges for the next film. "[We] had written ourselves into a corner at the end of *Far from Home* with Spider-Man's secret identity being revealed to the world by Mysterio," McKenna said.[2]

"So we had that as a starting point: how will Peter Parker deal with that [revelation]? And where would we go from there?" McKenna said. "There were a lot of conversations, a lot of different routes until the idea of the multiverse was opened up to us and made available as something we could play around with."[3]

McKenna and Sommers created a plot in which Peter Parker goes to Doctor Strange, played by Benedict

Cumberbatch, and pleads with him to use magic to make the world forget that he is Spider-Man. Strange agrees, but his spell goes wrong. The multiverse shatters, allowing villains from other universes to threaten the world.

CHANGES ON SET

Within days of wrapping *Uncharted* filming, Holland flew to Atlanta in November 2020 to start filming *No Way Home*. The world was still struggling with the COVID-19 pandemic, which forced filmmakers to adapt their plans. Some scenes that would have been simple to shoot in the past were now tricky to film.

Because of COVID-19 restrictions, only a limited number of people were allowed on set at the same time. This forced the team to rely more heavily on digitally created visual effects (VFX). "Before COVID, we planned a big New York location shoot with tons of extras," director Jon Watts said.[4]

"That became impossible. Even the most basic shot, of Peter Parker walking down the street, became a multilayered VFX shot," Watts said.[5] VFX artists started with footage of empty streets. Then they added layers of footage with extra actors to create the illusion of a crowded street.

Many scenes that would typically be shot on location were shot in front of a green screen, with backgrounds and details added digitally. For Holland, the experience was disappointing. His time shooting on location was limited, and he thought that affected how the film felt. The crew had to re-create various settings in the studio and then map out how each shot would work. In some scenes, Holland found this approach difficult.

THE END OF A TRILOGY

For Holland, filming *No Way Home* felt like the end of an era. He had been making *Spider-Man* films for five years and had developed close relationships with the cast and crew. "We were all treating [*No Way Home*] as the end of a franchise," he said. "I think if we were lucky

A REAL-LIFE FRIENDSHIP

In the *Homecoming* trilogy, Jacob Batalon plays Ned, Peter Parker's best friend. Off-screen, Batalon and Holland share a genuine friendship that began on the set of the first *Spider-Man* film. The pair shared a house in Atlanta while filming *Spider-Man: Homecoming,* which solidified the friendship. According to Batalon, the duo spent a lot of time eating junk food and having fun in the house. Through the years, Holland and Batalon have often been spotted joking around, traveling together, and supporting each other's careers.

In *No Way Home*, Doctor Strange's spell goes awry when Peter interrupts it, asking to modify the spell so that MJ, Ned, and Aunt May will still remember him.

enough to dive into these characters again, you'd be seeing a very different version. It would no longer be the *Homecoming* trilogy. We would give it some time and try to build something different and tonally change the films. Whether that happens or not, I don't know. But we were definitely treating [*No Way Home*] like it was coming to an end, and it felt like it."[6]

No Way Home hit theaters in December 2021. The film smashed previous records, becoming Sony Pictures' highest-grossing film. Earning more than $1.9 billion at the worldwide box office, *No Way Home* became the highest-grossing *Spider-Man* film in history. It is seventh on the list of the highest-grossing films of all time.[7] The movie received numerous award nominations, including an Academy Award nomination for Best Visual Effects.

SPIDER-MAN REUNION

Before *No Way Home*'s release, rumors had swirled about potential cameo appearances by past Spider-Man actors Tobey Maguire and Andrew Garfield. Fans were thrilled to see the two actors appear on-screen in the film to help Holland's Spider-Man. In the movie's finale, the three Spider-Men battle villains from the past, including Green Goblin, Lizard, and Sandman.

Holland said the fan reaction to Maguire and Garfield surprised him. "I always knew that this film would be loved around the world," Holland said in a joint interview with Maguire and Garfield. "I didn't think it would be quite as massive as it has been. One of my favorite things to do at the minute is to go online and watch fans' reactions to you guys coming in that one scene in particular. I don't think I could ever have imagined it as being so well received by everyone."[8]

"Myself, Andrew, Tobey—we have this amazing bond as three people who have been through something that is so unique that we really are like brothers."[9]

—Holland, 2023

Holland was also aware that *No Way Home* could be his last time playing Spider-Man. His initial agreement with Sony and Marvel had been fulfilled. "There definitely was a sense for me, as an actor, that this was the last time that I could potentially don the suit, so a lot of that emotion came from the act of saying goodbye, which is one of the biggest themes throughout this film," he said.[10]

This feeling was bolstered by the film's ending. Peter realizes the only way to save the world is by having Doctor Strange erase everyone's memories of him. This means MJ and Ned completely forget who Peter is.

While *No Way Home* left the future of Peter and MJ's relationship uncertain, Holland and costar Zendaya confirmed their romantic relationship in July 2021. Since then, the couple has attempted to keep the relationship private. They occasionally share social media posts and make public appearances together.

SECRETS AND LIES

Andrew Garfield's appearance in *Spider-Man: No Way Home* was such a highly guarded secret that the actor had to lie to his former Spider-Man costar Emma Stone about it. When Stone heard about the upcoming film, she texted Garfield to ask whether he was in the movie. He told her he didn't know what she was talking about. When Stone repeatedly asked, Garfield repeatedly lied, denying any involvement in the film. Garfield laughed at Stone's reaction after she finally saw the movie and learned the truth.

CHAPTER NINE

NEW VENTURES

Since the day Holland was chosen to be the next Spider-Man, his life had been a whirlwind. He had gone from a relatively unknown child actor to a beloved superhero recognized worldwide. His career was soaring, literally and figuratively. In January 2022, he decided to slow things down.

Holland joined the Dry January challenge, a popular sobriety challenge that many people attempt as part of their New Year's resolutions. The challenge involves not drinking alcohol for the entire month of January. Participants say Dry January helps them start the new year in a healthier way, prompting them to reexamine their relationship with alcohol.

Holland was surprised at how difficult it was for him to not drink alcohol. "I couldn't quite wrap my head around how much I was struggling without

Holland spoke about *The Crowded Room* at a 2023 screening in Los Angeles, California. >>

BERO LAUNCH

In 2024, Holland launched BERO, a nonalcoholic beer brand. After choosing to live an alcohol-free life, Holland found the available selection of nonalcoholic beers to be lacking. His brand offers several varieties, each named after something in Holland's life. Kingston Golden Pils is named after Holland's hometown, Kingston upon Thames. Edge Hill Hazy IPA bears the name of Holland's primary school, while Noon Wheat is named after Zendaya's dog, Noon.

booze in that first month—and it really scared me," he said. "I decided, as a sort of punishment to myself, that I would do February as well as January."[1]

February was even harder. Holland extended the challenge for another month. March was still a struggle, but he kept going. By June, he was starting to feel the benefits of sobriety. Without alcohol, he slept better, handled stress better, and maintained stronger relationships. By the following January, Holland decided to quit alcohol for good. "By the time I'd crossed that annual mark, I was done," he said. "I was like, 'I'm never gonna drink again because this is the best version of myself.'"[2]

THE CROWDED ROOM

Staying sober helped Holland with his next project, *The Crowded Room*. This limited television series aired on Apple TV+. The show follows Holland's character, Danny Sullivan, who is arrested for his involvement in a 1979 shooting. The role is dark, as the character is loosely based on the true story of Billy Milligan, who was diagnosed with a mental illness for his trial and claimed to have 24 alternate personalities.[3]

> "I'm quite strong-willed. When I decide to do something, I'm really gonna do it."[6]
>
> —Holland, on his decision to quit drinking alcohol, 2025

Milligan was the first person in the United States to be found not guilty for his crimes because of a mental disorder. Instead of going to prison, Milligan spent years in a psychiatric hospital. In addition to starring in the series, Holland also served as an executive producer.

The show's set was often a tense place to be. "There was quite a lot of animosity on that set. It was not a very harmonious place, and there was a lot of arguing and butting heads," Holland said.[4] Being sober helped the actor deal with the turmoil on set.

The first episodes of *The Crowded Room* premiered in June 2023. The show received mixed reviews. Despite the lukewarm reaction to the series, some critics praised Holland's performance. "This series belongs to Holland, and he's shattering to behold. His emotionally staggering performances take *The Crowded Room* to a whole new level," wrote critic Randy Myers.[5]

In *The Crowded Room*, Holland's Danny Sullivan is interviewed by a psychologist, who is played by Amanda Seyfried.

TAKING A BREAK

After *The Crowded Room*, Holland stepped back and took a break from acting. He had been working almost nonstop for years. The stress of filming *The Crowded Room* pushed the actor to his breaking point. The show's dark subject matter took a toll on Holland's mental health. "I'm no stranger to the physical aspects of the job, doing the whole action-movie thing," he said. "But the mental aspect, it really beat me up and it took a long time for me to recover afterwards, to sort of get back to reality."[7]

Several months into filming, there was one point when Holland could not free himself from Danny's character. One day, he had a meltdown and panicked at home.

He became convinced that he needed to shave his head to separate himself from Danny. Holland did not end up shaving his head since he was still in the middle of filming, but the experience left him shaken.

The series helped Holland realize the importance of caring for one's mental health. He decided to take a year-long break from acting. During his time off, Holland relaxed and spent time with his friends and family. He traveled, played golf, and even gardened. He did carpentry work around his house and played with the dogs he shares with Zendaya.

THE BROTHERS TRUST

In 2017, Holland and his family established a charitable foundation called the Brothers Trust. It supports and spotlights small charities that are often overlooked, especially those that focus on children's health, disability support, and education. The trust uses Holland's worldwide fame to raise awareness and funds through events, merchandise, and partnerships with corporations. The trust also hosts events to create memorable experiences for children living with physical and mental hardships.

RETURN TO THE STAGE

In May 2024, Holland emerged from his acting break and returned to London's West End in a stage adaptation of William Shakespeare's *Romeo and Juliet*. The show had a limited 12-week run through August 2024 at the

Duke of York's Theatre. Directed by Jamie Lloyd, the production starred Holland as Romeo and Francesca Amewudah-Rivers as Juliet.

Lloyd created a modern, minimalist version of the Shakespeare classic. The set featured a bare stage, a live-video-screen backdrop, and microphone stands. Fans were excited for Holland's return to the London stage, and tickets for the show's run sold out in just a few hours.

The play received mixed reviews from critics. Some praised the minimalist staging and applauded Holland's performance, while others thought the production lacked emotion. For Holland, returning to the London stage where his career began was a full-circle moment.

After the play's premiere, he posted a photo of the cast on Instagram and praised the production. "Tonight was the start of something so special. I'm beyond proud of our cast and crew who have gone above and beyond in every way," Holland wrote. "I can't wait for the rest of the run. Tonight was truly a highlight of my career, and I'm so glad I get to share it with these incredible people."[8]

BILLY17

In December 2024, Holland, his brother Harry, and producer Will South announced a new venture. The three

While playing Romeo in the West End production of *Romeo and Juliet*, Holland appeared on posters outside the Duke of York's Theatre.

men formed a production company, Billy17, and signed a deal with Sony Pictures to develop movies. The trio planned to launch the production company with an original project titled *Burnt*. Academy Award–winner Rodney Rothman signed on to write the screenplay.

"I've had an incredibly happy and successful relationship with Sony Pictures for almost a decade, so they felt like the perfect partner to launch our production company with," Holland said. "It's been an ambition of mine to take this step for some time now, and we're incredibly excited to bring entertaining and rewatchable movies to the big screen."[9]

A BRAND-NEW DAY

In March 2025, Sony announced that a new movie, *Spider-Man: Brand New Day*, would begin filming later in 2025 and was tentatively scheduled for release in July 2026. Holland would reprise his role as Peter Parker. Details on the plot and cast were sparse. But director Destin Daniel Cretton assured fans that he and his creative team were hard at work to develop the next chapter for the superhero.

Meanwhile, Holland was busy filming another project, director Christopher Nolan's adaptation of *The Odyssey*. Holland plays Telemachus in this classic Greek adventure story. The film, scheduled for a 2026 release, also stars Zendaya. Holland may also appear in a third major film in 2026, *Avengers: Doomsday*.

A HUMBLE SUPERSTAR

Since shooting to stardom as Spider-Man in 2016, Tom

Holland has teamed up with his brother Harry for charity events, film projects, and other ventures.

Holland has made millions of fans with his youthful energy and powerful performances. Off-screen, he has advocated for numerous charitable causes. The actor's authenticity and talent have made him a beloved figure in the MCU and in Hollywood. He has also continued to nurture his off-screen relationships. In January 2025, Holland and Zendaya's engagement was announced. The couple has expressed a desire to retire after starting a family.

FUTURE PROJECTS

In 2024, Billy17 announced plans to pursue several movie projects with Sony Pictures. One is a film adaptation of *The Rosie Project*, a best-selling novel by author Graeme Simsion, for Sony's TriStar Pictures. The company also plans to work with Sony's Amy Pascal to produce a film adaptation of *The Winner*, a novel by Teddy Wayne. Holland is set to star in the film.

Those who know Holland best say that he has not let fame change him. Director Joe Russo said, "He is hounded by the press. He's in a very high-profile relationship. And he has remained exactly the same through all of it. Completely genuine, completely earnest, and as lovable as he was the day he first walked into our office for his first audition."[10] With even more ambitious projects lined up for the future, Holland continues to cement his place as a talented performer and leader in the entertainment industry.

ESSENTIAL FACTS

Full Name: Thomas Stanley Holland

Date of Birth: June 1, 1996

Place of Birth: Kingston upon Thames, England

Parents: Dominic Holland and Nicola Holland

Education: Donhead Prep School, Wimbledon College, and BRIT School for Performing Arts and Technology

RISE TO STARDOM

- After training in dancing and acrobatics, 12-year-old Tom Holland landed his first acting role in London's West End production of *Billy Elliot: The Musical.*
- Holland was cast in *The Impossible*, which opened doors for small roles in other films.
- He landed the coveted role of Peter Parker, who is the hero Spider-Man, making Holland a worldwide star.

CAREER HIGHLIGHTS

- Holland was introduced as Spider-Man in *Captain America: Civil War*, earning the character a new place in the Marvel Cinematic Universe.
- He played Peter Parker in a stand-alone film, *Spider-Man: Homecoming*, and later its sequels *Far from Home* and *No Way Home*.
- The actor reprised his role as Spider-Man in two Avengers movies, *Avengers: Infinity War* and *Avengers: Endgame*.

- Holland earned praise for his performances in film and TV projects such as *Cherry*, *Uncharted*, and *The Crowded Room.*

MAJOR PLAYS, TV SHOWS, AND FILMS

- *Billy Elliot: The Musical* (2008–2010)
- *The Impossible* (2012)
- *Spider-Man: Homecoming* (2017)
- *Avengers: Infinity War* (2018)
- *Spider-Man: Far from Home* (2019)
- *Avengers: Endgame* (2019)
- *Cherry* (2021)
- *Spider-Man: No Way Home* (2021)
- *The Crowded Room* (2023)
- *Spider-Man: Brand New Day* (2026)

QUOTE

"When I read a script, I ask whether I've done it before. Is it a challenge? Is this something my parents would enjoy or even my grandparents would enjoy?"

—Tom Holland, 2021

GLOSSARY

acclaim
Enthusiastic praise.

acrobatic
Involving difficult or skillful physical movements, especially in gymnastics or the performing arts.

adamant
Refusing to be persuaded or to change one's mind.

agent
A person who represents an actress or actor and is in charge of getting them auditions for parts.

buoyant
Cheerful and optimistic.

charisma
Charm that inspires devotion in others.

covet
To greatly desire or seek after something.

dialogue
A conversation between two or more people, especially in a book, play, or movie.

emaciated
Abnormally thin or weak, especially because of illness or lack of food.

expedition
A journey undertaken for a specific purpose, often involving exploration or research.

franchise
A series of stories and associated media and products that share a setting, a story, or characters.

green screen
A filmmaking technique in which a solid-colored background is replaced digitally with images or scenery.

improvise
To make up dialogue and actions for a character on the spot without a written script.

mythical
Relating to creatures or events that are imaginary or fictional.

pandemic
An outbreak of disease over a large area.

post-traumatic stress disorder (PTSD)
A mental health condition brought on by a traumatic event.

prosthetic
An artificial body part used for special effects in movies and theater.

reprise
To repeat a performance or a song.

trajectory
The path or progression of something over time, such as a career.

wane
To decrease gradually in size, strength, or intensity.

ADDITIONAL RESOURCES

SELECTED BIBLIOGRAPHY

Franklin-Wallis, Oliver. "Tom Holland Is in the Center of the Web." *GQ*, 17 Nov. 2021, gq.com. Accessed 2 May 2025.

Khomami, Nadia. "From Billy Elliot to Spider-Man: How Tom Holland Won the World's Heart." *Guardian*, 24 Jan. 2022, theguardian.com. Accessed 2 May 2025.

Lang, Brent. "Tom Holland on 'Spider-Man: Homecoming,' Spinoffs and Planning for Bathroom Breaks." *Variety*, 27 Mar. 2017, variety.com. Accessed 10 Apr. 2025.

Larson, Lauren. "Tom Holland's New Superpower." *Men's Health*, 2 Jan. 2025, menshealth.com. Accessed 2 May 2025.

FURTHER READINGS

Edwards, Sue Bradford. *Spider-Man*. Abdo, 2026.

Marvel's Spider-Man: No Way Home the Official Movie Special Book. Titan Comics, 2023.

Sonneborn, Liz. *Zendaya*. Abdo, 2026.

ONLINE RESOURCES

To learn more about Tom Holland, please visit **abdobooklinks.com** or scan this QR code. These links are routinely monitored and updated to provide the most current information available.

MORE INFORMATION

For more information on this subject, contact or visit the following organizations:

THE BROTHERS TRUST

thebrotherstrust.org

The Brothers Trust is a charitable foundation established by Tom Holland and his family. It works to support charities that struggle to be heard. The organization's website features information about its latest fundraisers, events, and charitable efforts.

COMIC-CON MUSEUM

2131 Pan American Plaza
San Diego, CA 92101
comic-con.org/museum

The Comic-Con Museum celebrates comics, science fiction, fantasy, anime, video games, and other areas of pop culture. Marvel characters, including Spider-Man, are often featured.

UNIVERSAL ORLANDO RESORT

6000 Universal Blvd.
Orlando, FL 32819
universalorlando.com

The Islands of Adventure at the Universal Orlando Resort has a Marvel-themed area called Marvel Super Hero Island. Visitors can go on a Spider-Man ride, meet Marvel superheroes, and enjoy other activities there.

SOURCE NOTES

CHAPTER 1. THE ROLE OF A LIFETIME

1. Dana Noraas. "How Did Tom Holland Get the Role of Spider-Man?" *Collider*, 12 July 2023, collider.com. Accessed 30 June 2025.

2. Ramin Setoodeh. "Tom Holland Broke His Computer When He Found Out He Was Cast as Spider-Man." *Variety*, 20 Jan. 2021, variety.com. Accessed 30 June 2025.

3. Setoodeh, "Tom Holland Broke His Computer."

4. Setoodeh, "Tom Holland Broke His Computer."

5. "Tom Holland Cast as Marvel's New Spider-Man." *ABC4*, 27 Aug. 2015, abc4.com. Accessed 30 June 2025.

CHAPTER 2. EARLY YEARS

1. "Kingston upon Thames." *Britannica*, n.d., britannica.com. Accessed 30 June 2025.

2. "Billy Elliot: Awards." *Internet Movie Database*, n.d., imdb.com. Accessed 30 June 2025.

3. Nadia Khomami. "From Billy Elliot to Spider-Man: How Tom Holland Won the World's Heart." *Guardian*, 24 Jan. 2022, guardian.com. Accessed 30 June 2025.

4. Khomami, "From Billy Elliot to Spider-Man."

5. Khomami, "From Billy Elliot to Spider-Man."

6. Damian Whitworth. "This Girl Said 'It's Billy Elliot!' and Waved at Me." *Times*, 6 June 2005, thetimes.com. Accessed 30 June 2025.

7. Lucy Kane. "Being Billy Elliot." *Time & Leisure*, 15 Dec. 2021, timeandleisure.co.uk. Accessed 30 June 2025.

8. Oliver Franklin-Wallis. "Tom Holland Is in the Center of the Web." *GQ*, 17 Nov. 2021, gq.com. Accessed 30 June 2025.

9. "Billy Elliot the Musical." *London Theatreland*, n.d., london-theatreland.co.uk. Accessed 30 June 2025.

10. Kane, "Being Billy Elliot."

11. "Meet Billy Elliot: Tom Holland." *BETM TheSkyKid*, n.d., betm.theskykid.com. Accessed 30 June 2025.

12. Kane, "Being Billy Elliot."

13. Jonathan Dean. "Tom Holland Interview: Pirouetting His Way from Billy Elliot to Spider-Man." *Times*, 30 June 2019, thetimes.com. Accessed 30 June 2025.

CHAPTER 3. HOLLYWOOD'S CALLING

1. "Indian Ocean Tsunami of 2004." *Britannica*, 20 June 2025, britannica.com. Accessed 1 July 2025.

2. Claire Black. "Schoolboy Actor Tom Holland Finds Himself in Oscar Contention." *Scotsman*, 21 Dec. 2012, scotsman.com. Accessed 1 July 2025.

3. Dana Mathews. "Breakout Star Tom Holland on His Film Debut 'The Impossible.'" *Teen Vogue*, 22 Jan. 2013, teenvogue.com. Accessed 1 July 2025.

4. Nick Allen. "'The Impossible' Interview with Director Juan Antonio Bayona." *Scorecard Review*, 20 Dec. 2012, thescorecardreview.com. Accessed 1 July 2025.

5. Rebecca Ford. "Tom Holland on Staying Afloat in His Film Debut." *Hollywood Reporter*, 21 Dec. 2012, hollywoodreporter.com. Accessed 1 July 2025.

6. Black, "Schoolboy Actor Tom Holland Finds Himself in Oscar Contention."

7. "The Impossible (2012)." *Box Office Mojo*, n.d., boxofficemojo.com. Accessed 1 July 2025.

8. Justin Chang. "The Impossible." *Variety*, 10 Sept. 2012, variety.com. Accessed 1 July 2025.

9. Black, "Schoolboy Actor Tom Holland Finds Himself in Oscar Contention."

10. Ford, "Tom Holland on Staying Afloat in His Film Debut."

11. Jess Denham. "Tom Holland Describes Nausea-Inducing Whale Scene." *Independent*, 21 Dec. 2015, the-independent.com. Accessed 1 July 2025.

12. Adam Bentz. "Chris Hemsworth & Tom Holland's $94M Box Office Disappointment." *ScreenRant*, 8 Jan. 2025, screenrant.com. Accessed 1 July 2025.

CHAPTER 4. BECOMING SPIDER-MAN

1. Chris Cabin. "'Captain America: Civil War' Directors on Landing Spider-Man." *Collider*, 14 Jan. 2016, collider.com. Accessed 1 July 2025.

2. Rob Keyes. "Tom Holland Talks Spider-Man Costumes, Sequels, and Villains." *ScreenRant*, 3 Apr. 2017, screenrant.com. Accessed 1 July 2025.

3. Adam Chitwood. "Kevin Feige Confirms Peter Parker; Talks High School Spidey." *Collider*, 11 Apr. 2015, collider.com. Accessed 1 July 2025.

4. Ramin Setoodeh. "Tom Holland and Daniel Kaluuya on 'Spider-Man,' 'Black Panther.'" *Variety*, 20 Jan. 2021, variety.com. Accessed 1 July 2025.

5. "Civil War." *Box Office Mojo*, n.d., boxofficemojo.com. Accessed 1 July 2025.

6. Kwame Opam. "Spider-Man Is Amazing in Captain America: Civil War, But Has No Business Being in It." *Verge*, 7 May 2016, theverge.com. Accessed 1 July 2025.

7. David Crow. "Tom Holland Talks Breaking His Nose on The Lost City of Z." *Den of Geek*, 17 Oct. 2016, denofgeek.com. Accessed 1 July 2025.

8. "The Lost City of Z." *IMDb*, n.d., imdb.com. Accessed 1 July 2025.

CHAPTER 5. SWINGING TO STARDOM

1. Nick Vega. "Tom Holland Went Undercover in an NYC High School." *Business Insider*, 10 July 2017, businessinsider.com. Accessed 1 July 2025.

2. Rob Keyes. "Tom Holland Talks Spider-Man Costumes, Sequels, and Villains." *ScreenRant*, 3 Apr. 2017, screenrant.com. Accessed 1 July 2025.

3. Brent Lang. "Tom Holland on 'Spider-Man: Homecoming.'" *Variety*, 27 Mar. 2017, variety.com. Accessed 1 July 2025.

4. Lang, "Tom Holland on 'Spider-Man: Homecoming.'"

5. Lang, "Tom Holland on 'Spider-Man: Homecoming.'"

6. Joe Anderton. "Spider-Man Producer Advised Tom Holland and Zendaya Not to Date." *Digital Spy*, 20 Dec. 2021, digitalspy.com. Accessed 1 July 2025.

SOURCE NOTES

7. Seth Kelley. "'Spider-Man: Homecoming' Slings to Massive $117 Million Domestic Opening." *Variety*, 9 July 2017, variety.com. Accessed 1 July 2025.

8. Kelley, "'Spider-Man: Homecoming' $117 Million Domestic Opening."

9. "Homecoming." *Box Office Mojo*, n.d., boxofficemojo.com. Accessed 1 July 2025.

10. Benjamin Lee. "Spider-Man: Homecoming Review—Web-Slinging Wit Powers Razor-Sharp Reboot." *Guardian*, 29 June 2017, theguardian.com. Accessed 1 July 2025.

CHAPTER 6. MORE SPIDER-MAN

1. Zach Johnson. "Tom Holland on the Most 'Bizarre' Part of Filming Avengers: Infinity War." *E! News*, 25 Apr. 2018, eonline.com. Accessed 2 July 2025.

2. "Infinity War." *Box Office Mojo*, n.d., boxofficemojo.com. Accessed 2 July 2025.

3. Chris Agar. "Tom Holland Loved Shooting Spider-Man's *Infinity War* Death Scene." *ScreenRant*, 12 Feb. 2021, screenrant.com. Accessed 2 July 2025.

4. Dan Seddon. "Tom Holland Reveals How He Messed Up *Avengers: Endgame*'s Big Shot." *Digital Spy*, 22 Dec. 2021, digitalspy.com. Accessed 2 July 2025.

5. Sarah Whitten. "Disney's 'Avengers: Endgame' Shatters Box Office Records with $1.2 Billion Global Debut." *CNBC*, 29 Apr. 2019, cnbc.com. Accessed 2 July 2025.

6. "Top Lifetime Grosses." *Box Office Mojo*, 2 July 2025, boxofficemojo.com. Accessed 2 July 2025.

7. P. J. Rickards. "How Tom Holland Pulled Off His Own Stunts." *Business Insider*, 30 Mar. 2022, businessinsider.com. Accessed 2 July 2025.

8. Geoff Boucher. "Sony's 'Spider-Man: Far from Home' Trailer." *Deadline*, 18 Jan. 2019, deadline.com. Accessed 2 July 2025.

9. "All Time Worldwide Box Office for Sony Pictures Movies." *Numbers*, 2 July 2025, the-numbers.com. Accessed 2 July 2025.

CHAPTER 7. BEYOND THE WEB

1. Eli Countryman. "Tom Holland on 'The Devil All the Time.'" *Variety*, 11 Sept. 2020, variety.com. Accessed 3 July 2025.

2. Tom Brueggemann. "'Antebellum' Immediate #1 on VOD Charts While RBG Films Soar on Apple TV." *IndieWire*, 21 Sept. 2020, indiewire.com. Accessed 3 July 2025.

3. Michael Phillips. "'Devil All the Time' Review." *Chicago Tribune*, 11 Sept. 2020, chicagotribune.com. Accessed 3 July 2025.

4. Jonathan Heaf. "Tom Holland on His Darkest Role Yet." *GQ*, 15 Apr. 2021, gq.com. Accessed 3 July 2025.

5. Joseph Walsh. "Tom Holland Talks 'Painful' Preparation for 'Cherry.'" *Screen Daily*, 8 Feb. 2021, screendaily.com. Accessed 3 July 2025.

6. Walsh, "Tom Holland Talks 'Painful' Preparation for 'Cherry.'"

7. Peter Bradshaw. "Cherry Review—Taking the 'Post' Out of Post-Traumatic Stress Disorder." *Guardian*, 11 Mar. 2021, theguardian.com. Accessed 3 July 2025.

8. Walsh, "Tom Holland Talks 'Painful' Preparation for 'Cherry.'"

9. Oliver Franklin-Wallis. "Tom Holland Is in the Center of the Web." *GQ*, 17 Nov. 2021, gq.com. Accessed 30 June 2025.

10. Rollo Ross. "From Spider-Man to Nathan Drake." *Metro Philadelphia*, 13 Feb. 2022, metrophiladelphia.com. Accessed 3 July 2025.

11. Ross, "From Spider-Man to Nathan Drake."

12. "Uncharted." *Internet Movie Database*, n.d., imdb.com. Accessed 3 July 2025.

CHAPTER 8. BACK TO THE BIG SCREEN

1. Erik Davis. "Marvel's Kevin Feige on the MCU Multiverse, 'Far from Home' Post-Credits Scenes." *Fandango*, 7 July 2019, fandango.com. Accessed 3 July 2025.

2. "'Spider-Man: No Way Home' Co-Writers Talk Villains, Peter Parker & Changing the Script." *Credits*, 31 Dec. 2021, motionpictures.org. Accessed 3 July 2025.

3. "Villains, Peter Parker & Changing the Script."

4. Meg Dowell. "No Way Home Director Explains How COVID Forced VFX into the Most Basic Shots." *Comic Book Resources*, 28 Jan. 2022, cbr.com. Accessed 3 July 2025.

5. Dowell, "How COVID Forced VFX into the Most Basic Shots."

6. Devan Coggan. "Tom Holland Opens Up about Spider-Man: No Way Home." *Entertainment Weekly*, 14 Oct. 2021, ew.com. Accessed 3 July 2025.

7. "Top Lifetime Grosses." *Box Office Mojo*, 2 July 2025, boxofficemojo.com. Accessed 2 July 2025.

8. Pete Hammond. "Tom Holland, Tobey Maguire & Andrew Garfield Reunite to Talk Playing Spider-Man." *Deadline*, 26 Jan. 2022, deadline.com. Accessed 3 July 2025.

9. Seth Abramovitch. "Tom Holland Breaks Free." *Hollywood Reporter*, 14 June 2023, hollywoodreporter.com. Accessed 3 July 2025.

10. Hammond, "Holland, Maguire & Garfield Reunite."

CHAPTER 9. NEW VENTURES

1. Cara Lynn Shultz. "Tom Holland Says Dry January Pushed Him toward Sobriety." *People*, 18 Oct. 2024, people.com. Accessed 3 July 2025.

2. Shultz, "Holland Says Dry January Pushed Him toward Sobriety."

3. Paul Glynn. "Spider-Man Star to Take a Year-Long Break from Acting." *BBC*, 9 June 2023, bbc.com. Accessed 3 July 2025.

4. Lauren Larson. "Tom Holland's New Superpower." *Men's Health*, 2 Jan. 2025, menshealth.com. Accessed 3 July 2025.

5. Randy Myers. "'Crowded Room' a Gripping True-Crime Story." *Mercury News*, 9 June 2023, mercurynews.com. Accessed 3 July 2025.

6. Larson, "Tom Holland's New Superpower."

7. Emlyn Travis. "Tom Holland's Complex Role in *The Crowded Room*." *Entertainment Weekly*, 9 May 2023, ew.com. Accessed 3 July 2025.

8. "Tom Holland Calls *Romeo & Juliet* the 'Highlight of His Career.'" *Yahoo! News*, 14 May 2024, uk.news.yahoo.com. Accessed 3 July 2025.

9. Katcy Stephan. "Tom Holland Launches Billy17." *Variety*, 12 Dec. 2024, variety.com. Accessed 3 July 2025.

10. Larson, "Tom Holland's New Superpower."

INDEX

ABOUT THE AUTHOR

CARLA MOONEY

Carla Mooney is a graduate of the University of Pennsylvania. Today, she writes for young people and is the author of many books for young adults and children. She is an Avengers and Spider-Man fan and has seen most of the Marvel movies.